PLAYGROUND SURVIVAL

by Peggy Burns

Illustrated by Deborah Allwright

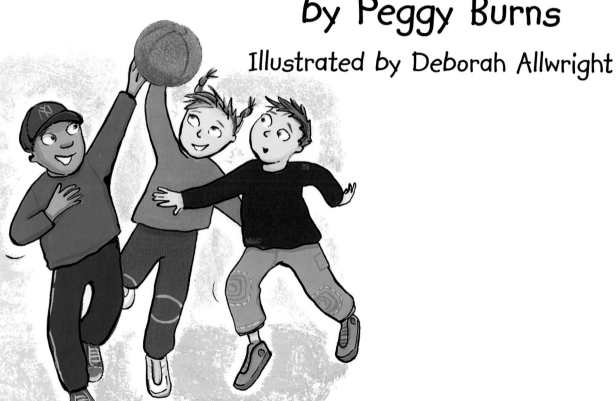

www.raintreepublishers.co.uk
Visit our website to find out more information about **Raintree** books.

To order:
 Phone 44 (0) 1865 888112
 Send a fax to 44 (0) 1865 314091
 Visit the Raintree bookshop at **www.raintreepublishers.co.uk** to browse our catalogue and order online.

First published in Great Britain by Raintree,
Halley Court, Jordan Hill, Oxford OX2 8EJ,
part of Harcourt Education.
Raintree is a registered trademark of Harcourt Education Ltd.

Raintree Editor: Kate Buckingham
Series Consultant: Dr Michele Elliott, Kidscape
Written by Peggy Burns
Illustrated by Deborah Allwright
Packaged by ticktock Media Ltd.
Designed by Robert Walster, BigBlu Design
Edited and project managed by Penny Worms

Printed and bound in China, by South China Printing

ISBN 1 844 43417 6
08 07 06 05 04
10 9 8 7 6 5 4 3 2 1 .

British Library Cataloguing in Publication Data
Burns, Peggy
Playground survival. – (Kids' Guides)
302.3'4
A full catalogue record for this book is available from the
British Library.

CONTENTS

INTRODUCTION

Going to school can make life fun. There are so many exciting things to do: games to play, interesting things to learn, new friends to make. But great as school can be, things don't always run smoothly. It is good to have friends to play with. But even best friends can become **jealous**, or start teasing each other, or say hurtful things.

Not everyone finds it easy to make friends in the first place. Perhaps you are finding that other children do not want to play with you. It could be because you are **shy** or because you are different from them in some way. They might not know you, yet they have made up their minds not to like you. This can be upsetting, and you can end up feeling unhappy and lonely.

This book will show you that any playground problem has a solution, and it begins with talking about what's wrong. Try it – it really works!

Let's talk about...
FRIEND TROUBLES

It is great to have friends. You always have someone to talk to, play with and share secrets with. Friends are there for the good times, and help each other through the bad times, but even best friends **quarrel**. Your friend shouts at you; you shout back. You both say unkind things and before you know it you have fallen out.

BUT WHY ME?

Everyone gets on with some people more than others. Friends may argue, they may even fight, but if someone is nasty to you a lot of the time, he or she is not a true friend.

That's not fair.

You cheated.

You are not the only ones – children everywhere fall out with each other all the time. Making up can be difficult, especially if you both think the other is in the wrong! It helps to:

● smile at your friend so they know you are not still angry

● say you are sorry to each other

● talk about it and then move on to become friends again.

LOOK AT IT ANOTHER WAY

If you have fallen out, you are probably thinking more about how you feel. But your friend is probably feeling just as unhappy. Saying sorry is never easy, but being friends again is well worth it!

Let's talk about...
BEING DIFFERENT

How boring the world would be if everyone were the same. No two people in the world are exactly alike. Even identical twins have different interests and talents. You may be confident or **shy**, tall or short, black or white, or you may like football – or hate it!

Some people turn against others because they are different or have different interests. This is called **prejudice**.

You can play but not your friend.

Then I won't play thanks!

He's prejudiced.

BUT WHY ME?

It is very unfair when people make up their minds that they don't like you before they know you. You can't help how other people think, but you can decide that their prejudice is not going to hurt you.

Prejudiced people take a dislike to someone for no good reason. They may judge a person before they know them. They may think they are better than you. Perhaps they call you nasty names or refuse to make friends with you.

WHY DO I FEEL LIKE THIS?

If someone is making you feel unwanted, ugly, or unimportant, they are in the wrong — not you. If they weren't being nasty to you, you wouldn't be feeling this way.

9

Those girls are rude...but that's their problem.

Being treated unfairly makes you feel angry, sad and hurt, but remember:

● they are the ones with the problem, not you

● walk away rather than let them see they have upset you

● everyone is important and special

● never allow yourself to believe the things prejudiced people say about you.

LOOK AT IT ANOTHER WAY

People usually think the same things as their parents and family. They might be prejudiced because of the way they have been brought up. Their views can be changed.

Let's talk about...
SCHOOL BULLIES

Being bullied is the worst thing to deal with in the playground. A bully might hit you, pull your hair, or take your things. He or she might spread **rumours** about you, or say nasty things to you. They might ignore you and get others to refuse to speak to you.

WHY DO I FEEL LIKE THIS?

Being bullied is very upsetting. Bullies make you feel lonely, sad, angry — and very scared.

Why won't they leave me alone?

BUT WHY ME?

People are bullied because the bully has a problem. The bully may say it is because you are small or tall, thin or fat, black or white, poor or rich — but it is really about the bully looking for ways to hurt someone.

Sometimes people who are *bullied* believe what the bully says and feel bad about themselves. This makes the bully feel that he or she has won.

11

I must be doing something wrong.

If you are *bullied*, it is NOT your fault, it is the bully's fault. So remember:
● you are not to blame
● you do not deserve to be picked on for any reason
● you should feel safe and happy
● all bullying is wrong, and telling an adult is the only way to make it stop.

I've got to tell someone.

LOOK AT IT ANOTHER WAY

Bullies are often unhappy deep down inside. They may be **jealous** of the people they bully or they do it because they have been bullied themselves. Whatever the reason, bullies have to be stopped, but they may need help, too.

True stories

THREE'S A CROWD

Hi there. I'm Ellie. Sheema has been my best friend for a long time. We started school on the same day! Recently a new family moved into our street, and I made friends with Hannah.

I hate playing on my own.

After the holidays Hannah joined our class, and all three of us – me, Sheema and Hannah – all played together. But Sheema and Hannah started to leave me out. I didn't know why.

Then someone told me that Sheema was spreading a **rumour** about me. She told everyone my Dad left home because he doesn't love me or my mum any more. Everyone thinks it's true! I'm really upset. Sheema knows that my Dad is working in Germany. He's coming home at Christmas.

THREE'S A CROWD

Talking it through

It helps to talk to someone...

A BROTHER

Ellie's brother Luke can not understand why Ellie's best friend would hurt her like that. He advises Ellie to talk to Sheema and try to find out why she has made up such a story.

A PARENT

Ellie writes to her dad and tells him what has happened. He is rather cross! He writes back and tells Ellie that she should take his letter to school and show it to her friends.

A PARENT

Ellie's mum wonders what could have made Sheema spread such a **rumour**. She says Sheema must have her reasons. She offers to have a quiet word with Sheema's mum.

FORWARD STEPS

● **TALK**
Don't keep problems bottled up inside you.

● **SHARE**
You can *be* friends with more than one person. The more friends you have the *better*.

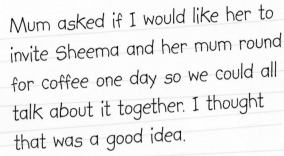 

Mum asked if I would like her to invite Sheema and her mum round for coffee one day so we could all talk about it together. I thought that was a good idea.

Sheema went red and said she was **jealous** when I'd become friendly with Hannah. She didn't want to share her best friend with anyone, so she told lies about me hoping that Hannah wouldn't want me as a friend any more. She was really **ashamed** of what she'd done, and said she was sorry. She told people at school about it as well, which must have been very hard. I took Dad's letter to school – with a photo of Dad working on his building site. He'd sent German sweets, too, which I shared with my whole class!

True stories

HE'S A WEIRDO

Hi, my name is Robert. I recently started at a new school. I was a bit nervous at first because I have **epilepsy**. It doesn't worry me, because I take medicine that controls it. I do sometimes have a **seizure**, but the teacher told the class about it so I thought everything would be fine.

I don't remember a thing.

I quickly got to know people, and made friends with Luke. Then one day I had an attack in the playground. My attacks don't last long, but Mum says they are frightening to watch. I scream, then fall down and jerk about.

After that, people didn't want to be friends with me any more. Luke said I was freaky. And I thought he was my friend! Why are they afraid of me? I'm no weirdo.

HE'S A WEIRDO Talking it through

It helps to talk to someone...

A SISTER

Robert's big sister, Kate, reminds him that thousands of people have **epilepsy**. She says he should explain to the kids at school about epilepsy, and tell them that there's nothing freaky about having any illness.

A PARENT

Dad says that Robert should feel good about himself because he is coping so well with having epilepsy. He says he will go to Robert's school and have a chat with his teacher.

A TEACHER

Mr Harris has already told the class about Robert's illness, but realizes that they need to know more. He tells Robert not to worry, he will organize a class discussion.

FORWARD STEPS

- **TELL YOUR TEACHER**
It is important that teachers know if you have an illness, so that they can help classmates to understand.

- **BE CONFIDENT**
Having an illness or disability of any kind does not make anyone a weirdo!

I was glad I'd told my family about it because Dad went and talked to Mr Harris. That same day Mr Harris told the class that I might have a **seizure** again. He said that it might be a bit upsetting, but there was nothing freaky about having epilepsy, and nothing to be scared of. We had a discussion about it so that everyone could learn what it was like to have epilepsy. He said that nobody should be picked on because they have an illness.

At playtime Luke apologized for calling me names. We're best friends now. And when I had another seizure a few weeks later, Luke took charge – he was brilliant!

Are you okay now?

Yes, thanks Luke.

True stories

THE SCHOOL BULLY

Hello, my name is Andreas. My dad is English, and my mum was Italian. They **divorced** when I was little, and I lived with my mum in Italy. But last spring she died. That was horrible. Then I came to live with my dad in England. I am learning to speak English, but I am not very good at it yet. I go to the local primary school, but I don't like it because of Dwayne and his mates.

Oh no! Here they come.

Tell anyone and we will get you!

They make fun of my Italian **accent**, trip me up and take my things. The other day, Dwayne grabbed my PE shirt and stuffed it down the loo. He said that if I tell anyone they will beat me up. I'm too scared to go to school, so I have told my dad I feel sick. I know he doesn't believe me.

THE SCHOOL BULLY

Talking it through

It helps to talk to someone...

A FRIEND

Josh sits next to Andreas at school, and he has seen for himself the way that Dwayne and his gang are bullying him. He tells Andreas he should talk to a grown-up about it who will help to make them stop.

A PARENT

Andreas's dad is pleased he's talked to him. He tells him that grown-ups can help with problems, but only if they are told about them. He says he'll go to school to talk to Andreas's teacher.

A TEACHER

Miss Rees is sad to hear that Andreas is being bullied. She tells him not to be scared of Dwayne any more, because she is going to make sure that the bullying stops for good.

FORWARD STEPS

● **BE DETERMINED**
Don't allow bullies to rule your life.

● **TELL SOMEONE**
If you are being bullied, you should tell a grown-up you can trust. Bullies must be made to stop hurting you, and they need help too.

I wasn't going to be bullied by anyone ever again.

So you know how horrible it feels, Dwayne.

I hadn't wanted to tell Dad about Dwayne and his gang. I didn't want to get beaten up! And I thought that if Dad talked to Miss Rees it might make things worse. But I agreed, and now I'm glad because everything turned out fine. In class we talked about why people bully, and how people who are bullied feel. Everybody joined in. Dwayne told us how he was bullied at his last school. He said that when he came here he decided that he wasn't going to be bullied any more – he turned into a bully instead.

Nowadays, I enjoy school because I'm not scared any more. Dwayne leaves me alone and my English is getting better all the time.

True stories

GREEN-EYED MONSTER

Hi there, I'm Daisy. Not long ago we moved house, and I started going to a different school. Ruth sits next to me in class. Last week she invited me to her birthday disco. I wanted to go, but I had no money for a present or a card, because my dad's out of work just now.

I hope she likes it.

Mum said I should make Ruth a card, so I painted a picture of a fairy sitting on a flower, and wrote 'Happy birthday, Ruth' on it.

Look, Mum. Another Barbie!

At the party I realized that Ruth's parents are rich. I was really **embarrassed** about my homemade card! Everyone had brought her a present. The best one was a beautiful Barbie with long shiny hair and lots of clothes. Suddenly I hated Ruth for having everything she wants. Why do we have to be poor?

Talking it through

It helps to talk to someone...

A GRANDPARENT

Daisy's grandad says he understands how she feels. He tells her to be **patient** for a while longer because he is sure that her dad will get a job soon. After that, things should get better.

A SISTER

Daisy's sister Alison cuddles her and tells her not to turn into a 'green-eyed monster'. She says it is the name given to **envious** people and that it wasn't right to dislike someone just because they've got nice things.

A FRIEND

Her friend, Ruth, tells Daisy that what a person is like inside is more important than having money and lots of toys. She thinks it is better to be nice than rich – and Daisy is very nice!

FORWARD STEPS

● BE POSITIVE

Try not to be envious when friends have things that your parents can't afford. Envy can take over your thoughts if you let it!

● VALUE YOURSELF

Even if you are poor, you can make sure that you are a nice person.

We can't help the family we are born into.

We should appreciate the one we have!

On the next school day, Ruth thanked me for the birthday card. She said that she thought mine was the nicest she'd had, because I'd made it just for her! So I stopped feeling **ashamed** that it was homemade.

After the party I'd felt very **jealous** of Ruth. It didn't seem fair that she had four Barbies when I didn't even have one! But talking about it helped a lot. I know now that I was wrong to judge Ruth because her family is well-off. I think Ruth was right when she said it's more important to be a nice person than it is to be rich.

And yesterday, Dad went for an **interview** for a job. I hope he gets it!

Quiz

WHAT WOULD YOU DO?

1. What would you do if someone at school is telling lies and spreading **rumours** about you?

a) Decide that you will never speak to that person again.

b) Start spreading a rumour about them, to show them how horrible it is.

c) Try to find out why he or she would want to make others believe something that isn't true.

d) Not say anything about it, and wait for everyone to forget the rumour.

2. What would you do if, like Robert, people call you names because you have an illness that makes you seem different from them?

a) Make sure that your friends understand about your illness.

b) Stay in the background and hope that the bullying will stop.

c) Think up a few bad names that you can call them.

d) Wait for them to get tired of picking on you.

3. What would you do if, like Andreas, you are being bullied?

a) Run away.

b) Keep quiet about it, hoping the bully will leave you alone and pick on someone else.

c) Talk to a grown-up about it.

d) Learn to fight back.

4. What would you do if you feel **envious** of a friend whose parents can afford to give her whatever she wants?

a) Decide that she must be stuck-up, because all rich people are snobs.

b) Get angry with your own parents and complain about being poor.

c) Feel sorry for yourself. It's not fair!

d) Decide that nobody deserves to be disliked because of how much money they have or haven't got.

I don't remember a thing.

Answers

That's not fair.

You cheated.

1.c) There are always reasons why people act as they do. It is important to talk things over and find out why they are telling lies about you. Then you can find a solution to the problem.

2.d) People need to know how your illness affects you!

3.c) Always tell a grown-up if you are being bullied. Bullies need to be stopped – and maybe even helped.

4.d) None of us can choose the family we are born into but we should all **appreciate** the one we have. Your family might or might not be well-off at the moment, but things can change in the future.

Glossary

accent
the way a person pronounces words

appreciate
value something you have

ashamed
feeling upset because of the way you have behaved

disability
handicap that makes someone unable to do something

divorced
when a marriage is legally ended

embarrassed
when someone feels self-conscious and awkward

envy or envious
feeling jealous when another person has things you would like

epilepsy
disease that causes someone to have seizures (fits)

interview
a talk, often between an employer and a person looking for work, to find out whether he or she is suitable for a job

jealousy or jealous
the feeling of wanting to be like someone else because the other person is better in some way

patient
remain calm in difficult situations

prejudice
judge another person before knowing them or knowing all the facts

rumour
story that is passed around which may not be true

quarrel
argue or disagree

seizure
sudden fit, or an attack of illness

shy
not confident; if you are shy you find it difficult to talk to other people

Find out more

USEFUL BOOKS

All About Bullying by Lesley Ely

A book for older readers that will help you if you're being bullied.

All for One by Jill Murphy

A picture book about a monster excluded from his friends' games.

Everyone I See is Luckier Than Me by Clare Bevan

Poems about being jealous and how to overcome it.

Problem Solvers by Janine Amos

A series of stories showing how to deal with conflict at school.

Willy The Champ by Anthony Browne

Billy is laughed at because he is different, but when he gets threatened by the school bully, he shows how strong he is.

USEFUL WEBSITES

www.bbc.co.uk/cbbc/yourlife

A fun site about growing up, including how to deal with bullies.

www.kidshealth.org

Information for parents and children on feelings and how to deal with them.

www.pbskids.org

Stories for three to seven year olds and resources for parents on staying safe and feeling good about school and friends.

www.kidshelp.com.au

A general helpline for children.

USEFUL CONTACTS

Childline

Freepost 1111, London N1 0BR

Helpline: 0800 1111

www.childline.org.uk

For those children who need to talk to someone outside of their families.

Kidscape

2 Grosvenor Gardens, London, SW1W 0DH

Helpline: 08451 205204

www.kidscape.org.uk

Helps children being bullied or hurt.

Index